Flags Of the World

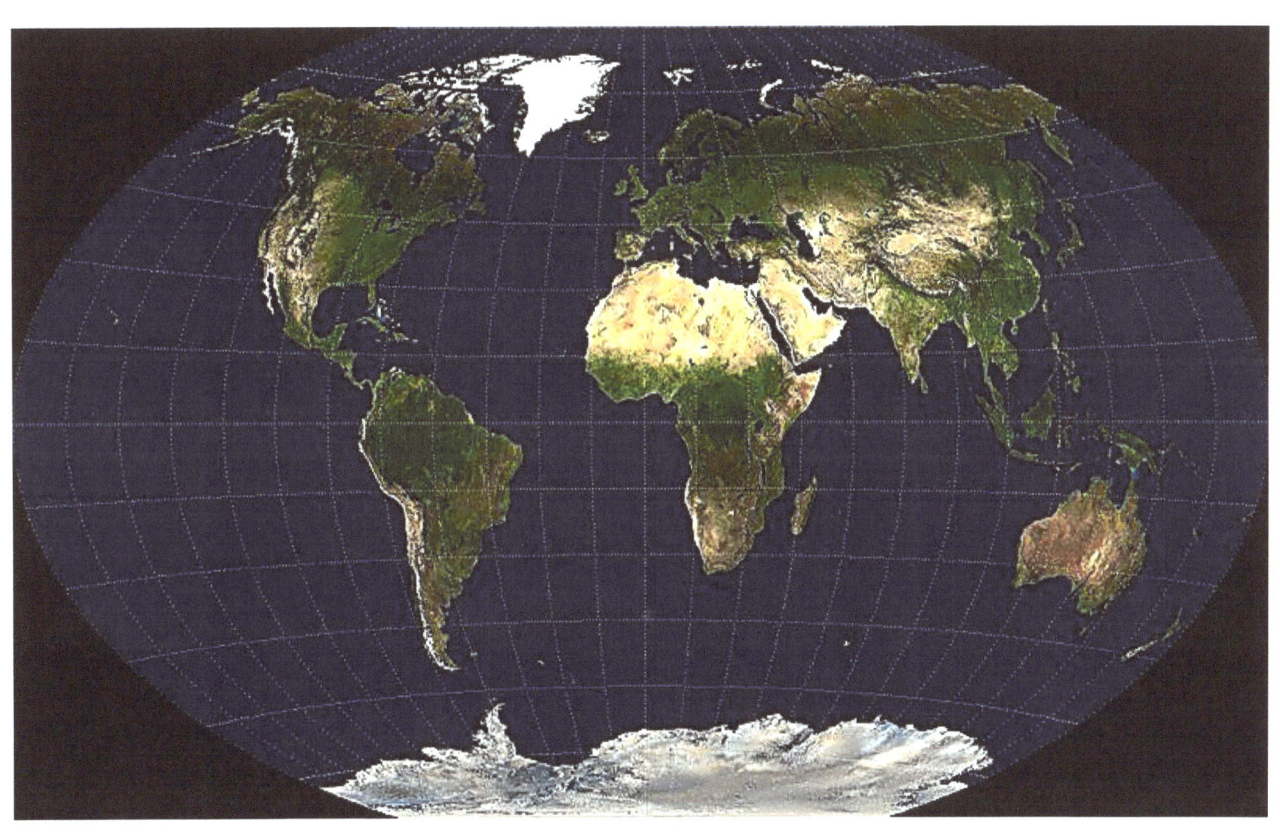

Catherine McGrew Jaime

Creative Learning Connection

8006 Old Madison Pike, Ste 11-A
Madison, Alabama 35758
U.S.A.

www.CreativeLearningConnection.com

Introduction

Flags are a great way to learn about the geography of the world!

You will find common elements in many of the flags, and many that are quite unique.

Enjoy the flags; study the colors and the symbols that have been used for centuries. Do you see trends within continents? What is the most common shape? The most unusual? Which countries use words on their flags? What colors are used most commonly? What other distinctions do you find?

Flags

of Africa

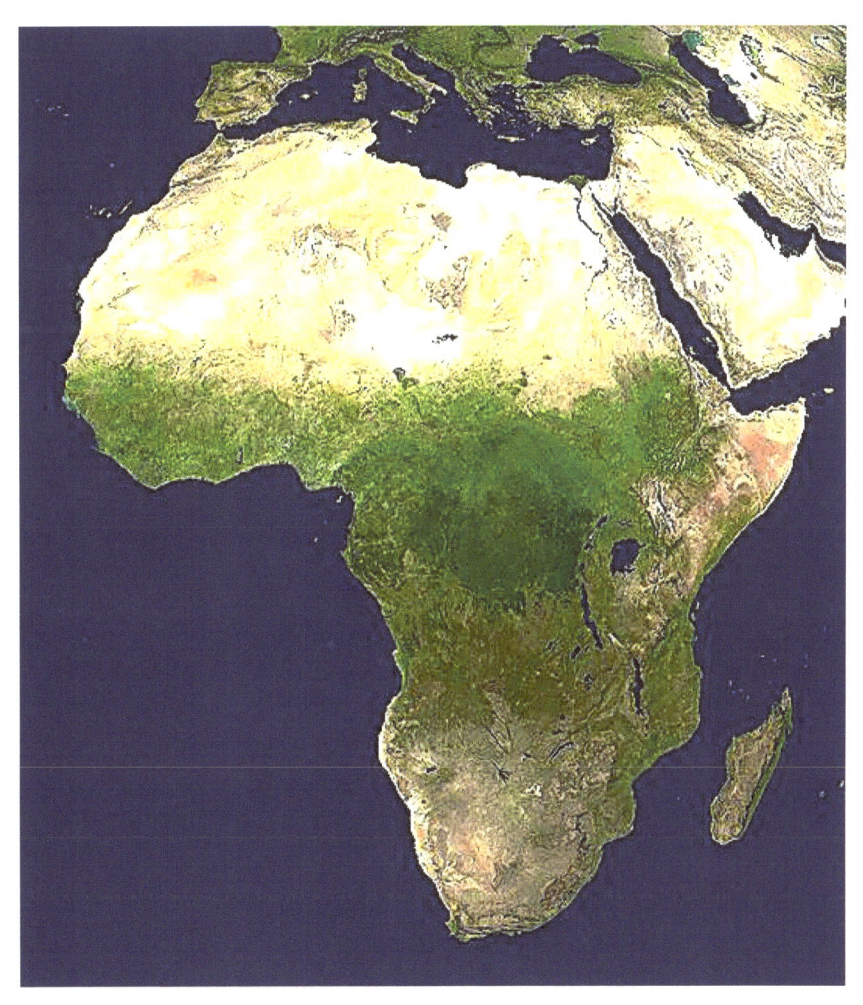

Algeria	Angola	Benin
Botswana	Burkina Faso	Burundi
Cameroon	Cape Verde	Central African Republic

Chad

Comoros

Congo

Côte
d'Ivoire

Democratic
Republic of
the Congo

Djibouti

Egypt

Eritrea

Equatorial
Guinea

Ethiopia

Gabon

Gambia

Ghana

Guinea

Guinea-
Bissau

Kenya

Lesotho

Liberia

Libya

Madagascar

Malawi

Mali

Mauritania

Mauritius

Morocco

Mozambique

Namibia

Niger

Nigeria

Rwanda

São Tomé
and Príncipe

Senegal

Seychelles

Sierra
Leone

Somalia

South
Africa

Sudan

Swaziland

Tanzania

Togo

Tunisia

Uganda

Zambia

Zimbabwe

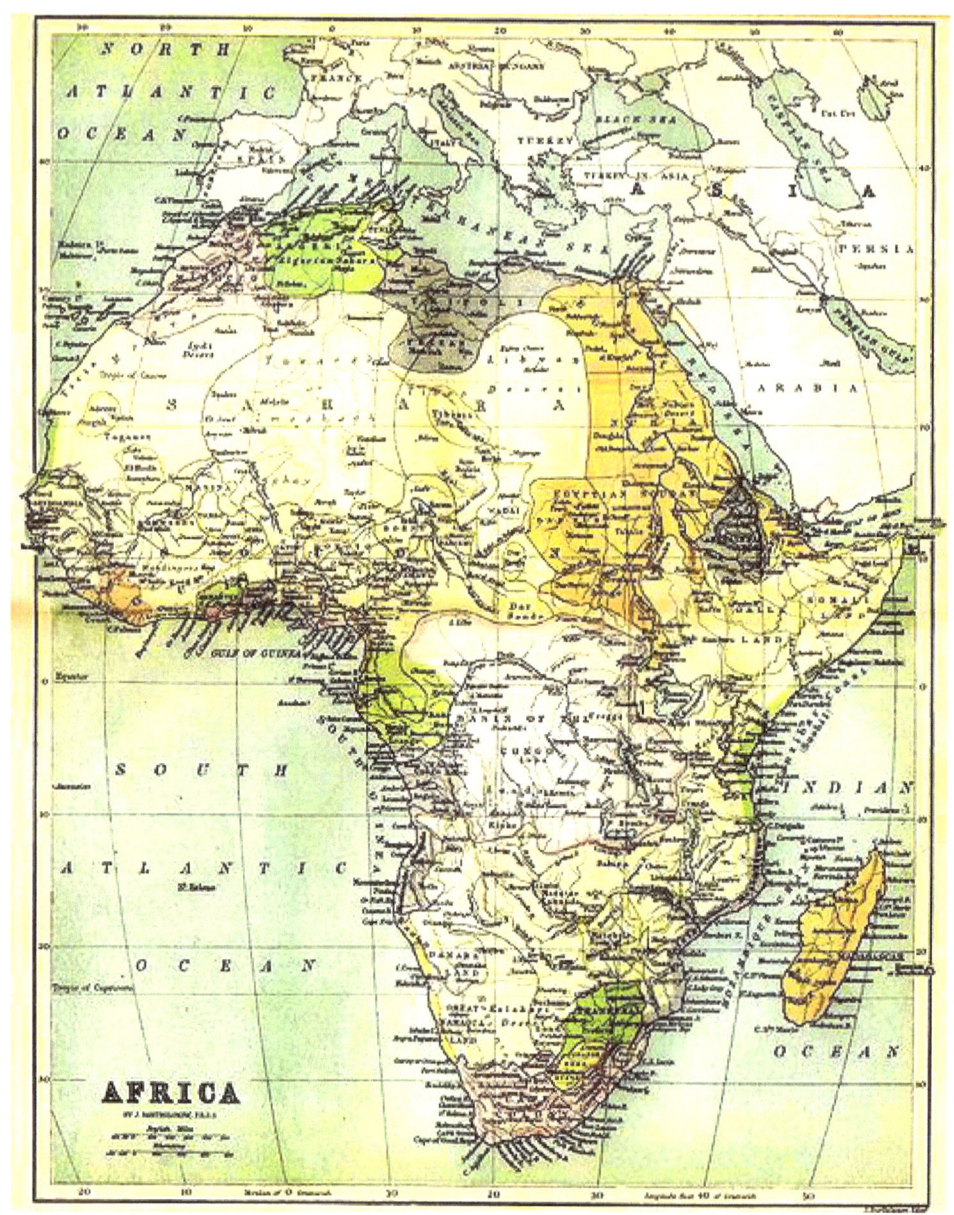

1885 Map of Africa

Flags

of Asia

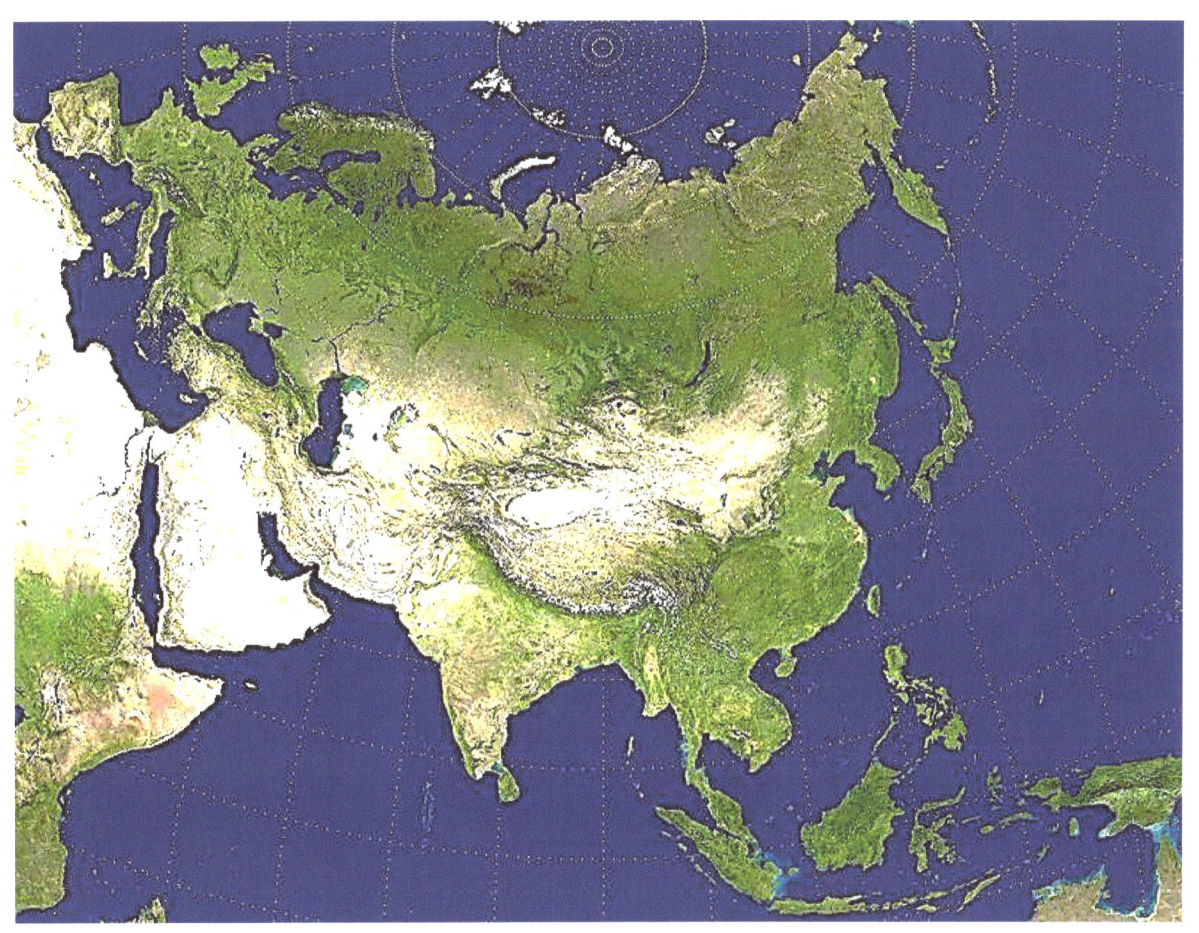

Afghanistan

Armenia

Azerbaijan

Bahrain

Bangladesh

Bhutan

Brunei

Cambodia

China

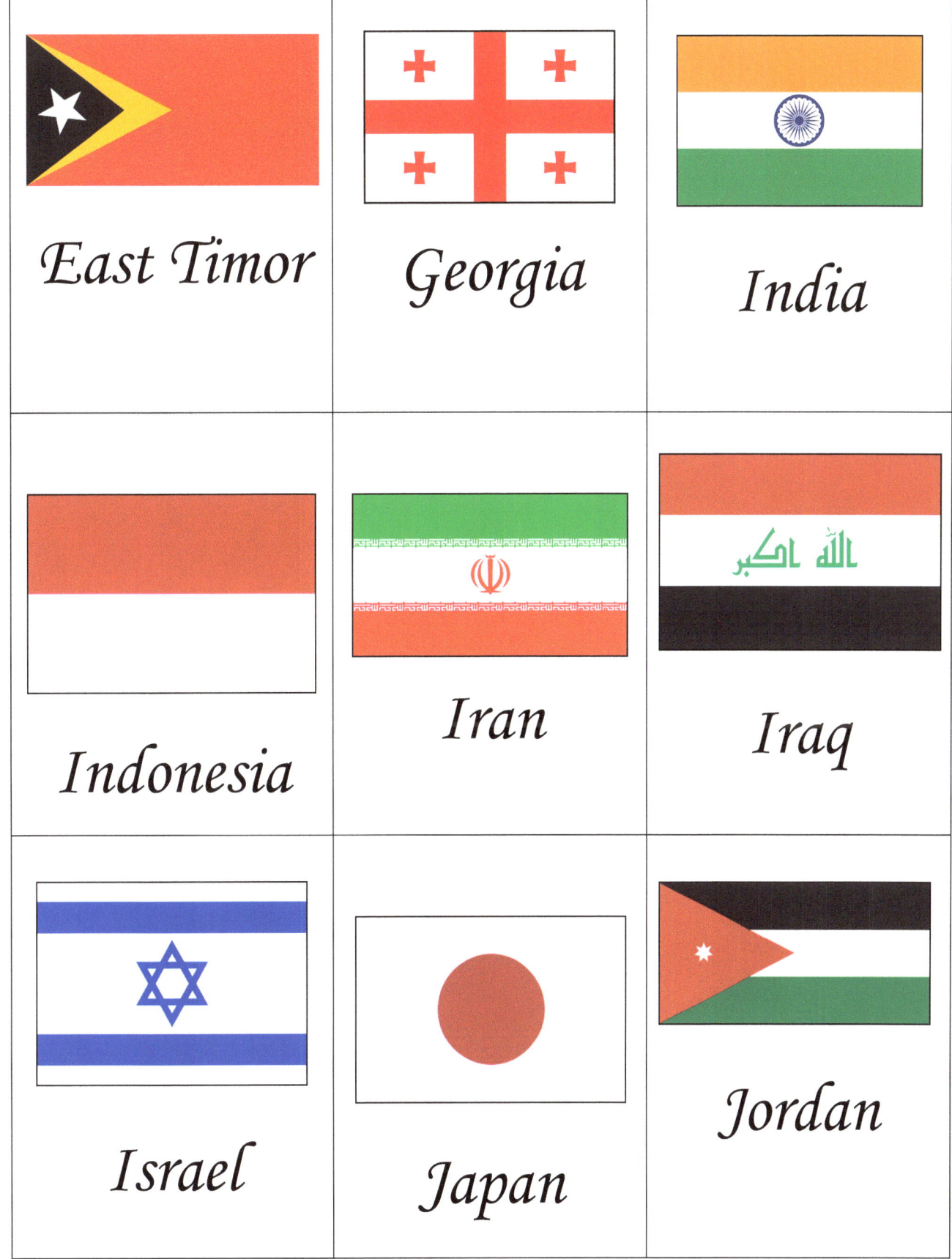

East Timor

Georgia

India

Indonesia

Iran

Iraq

Israel

Japan

Jordan

Kazakhstan

Kuwait

Kyrgyzstan

Laos

Lebanon

Malaysia

Maldives

Mongolia

Nepal

North Korea	Oman	Pakistan
Philippines	Qatar	Russia
Saudi Arabia	Singapore	South Korea

Sri Lanka

Syria

Taiwan

Tajikistan

Thailand

Turkey

Turkmenistan

United Arab
Emirates

Uzbekistan

Vietnam

Yemen

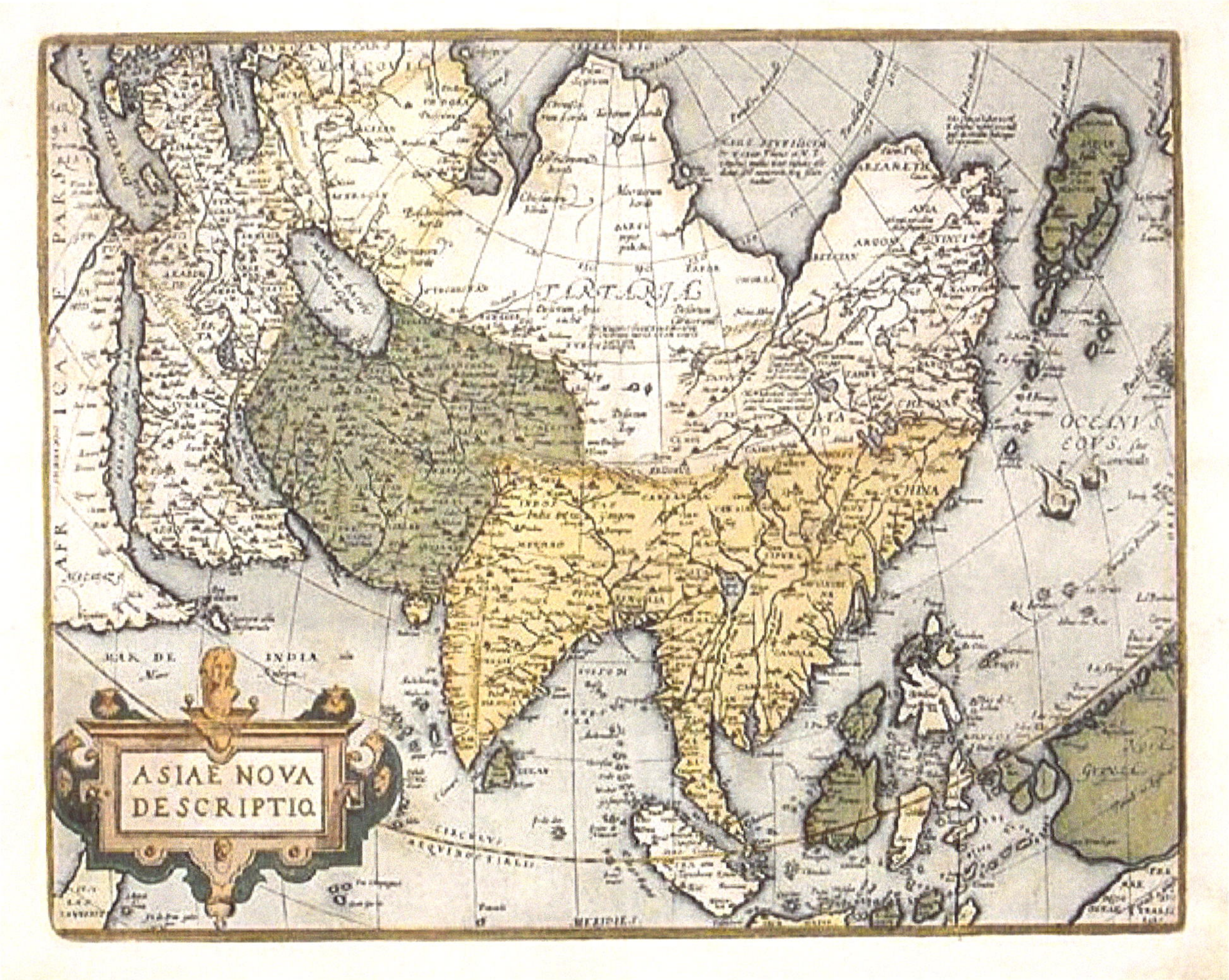

1595 Map of Asia

Flags in Art

Self-Portrait by
Henri Rousseau, 1890

Flags

of Europe

Albania	Andorra	Armenia
Austria	Azerbaijan	Belarus
Belgium	Bosnia & Herzegovina	Bulgaria

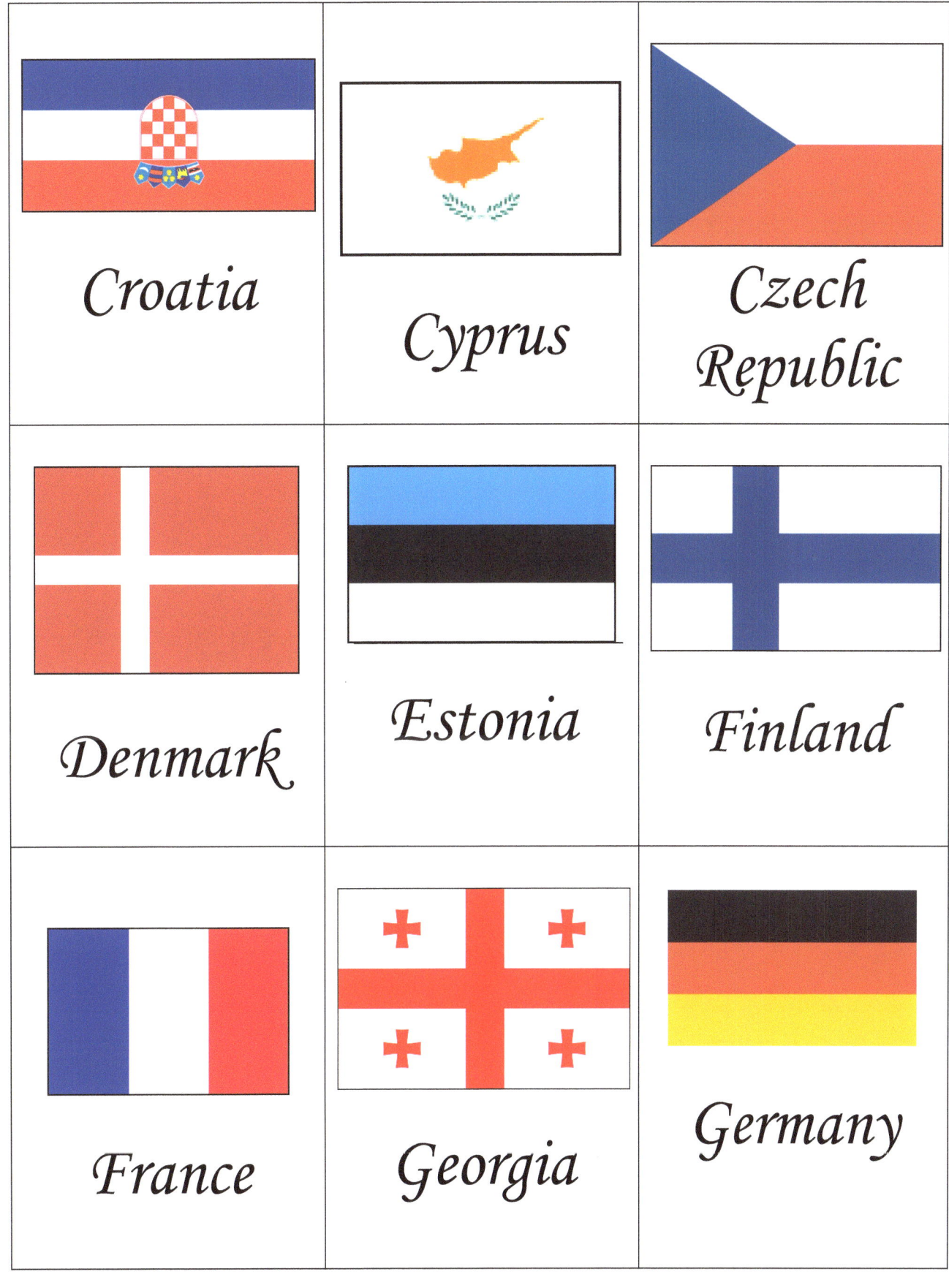

Croatia

Cyprus

Czech Republic

Denmark

Estonia

Finland

France

Georgia

Germany

Greece

Hungary

Iceland

Ireland

Italy

Kazakhstan

Latvia

Liechtenstein

Lithuania

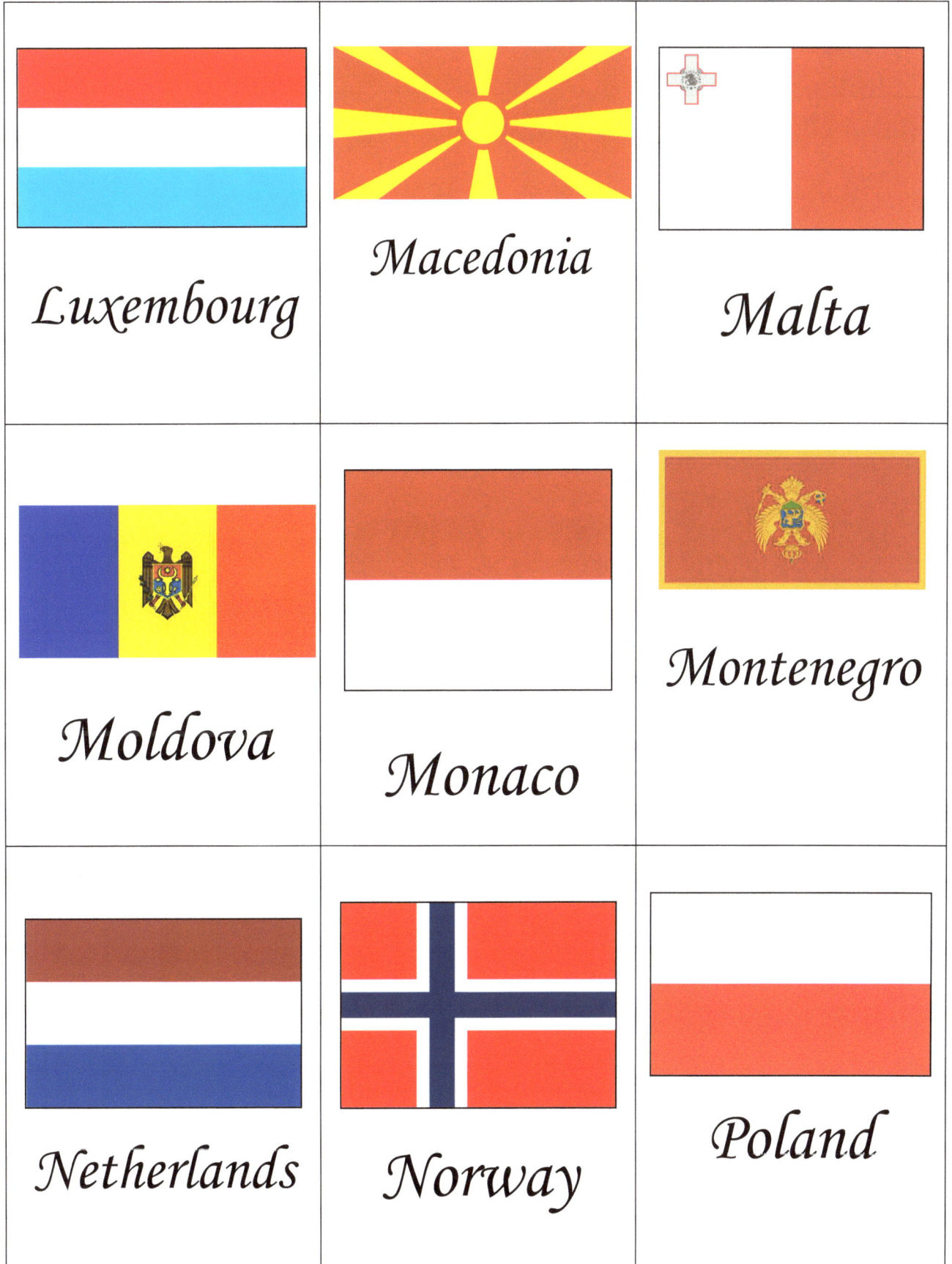

Luxembourg

Macedonia

Malta

Moldova

Monaco

Montenegro

Netherlands

Norway

Poland

Portugal

Romania

Russia

San Marino

Serbia

Slovakia

Slovenia

Spain

Sweden

Switzerland

Turkey

Ukraine

United
Kingdom

Vatican City

1594 Map of Europe

Flags

of North America

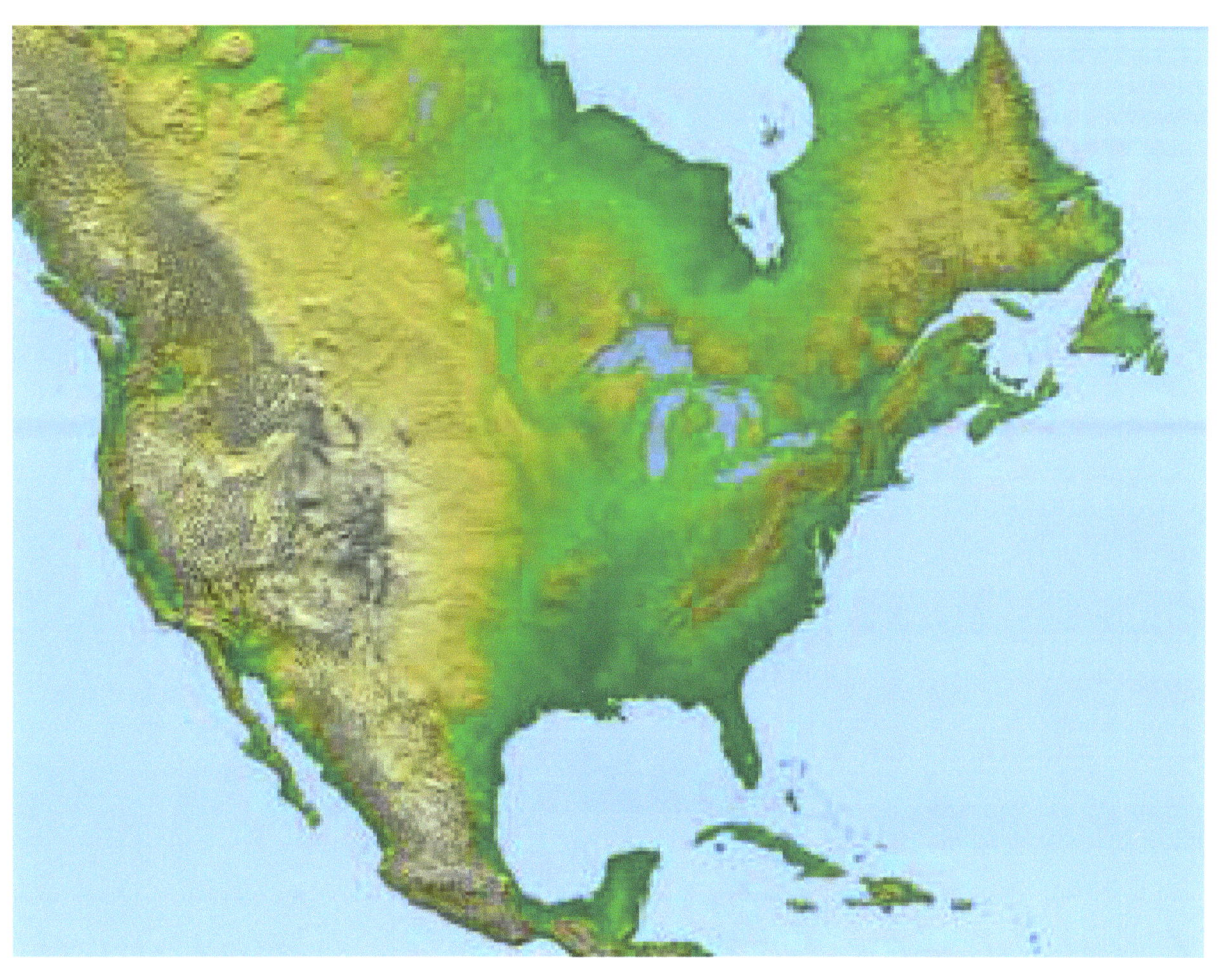

Canada

Greenland

Mexico

United States

Countries of Central America:

Belize

Costa Rica

El Salvador

Guatemala

Honduras	Nicaragua	Panama
Countries of the Caribbean:	Antigua and Barbuda	Bahamas
Barbados	Cuba	Dominica

Dominican Republic

Grenada

Haiti

Jamaica

Saint Kitts and Nevis

Saint Lucia

Saint Vincent and the Grenadines

Trinidad and Tobago

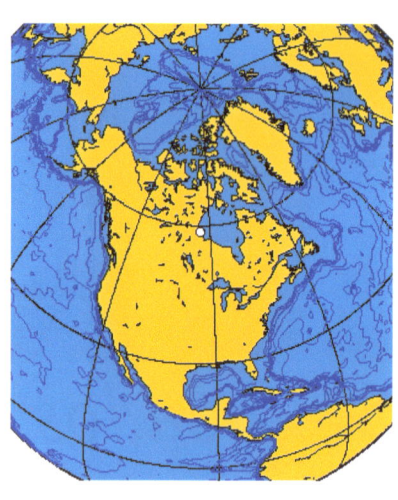

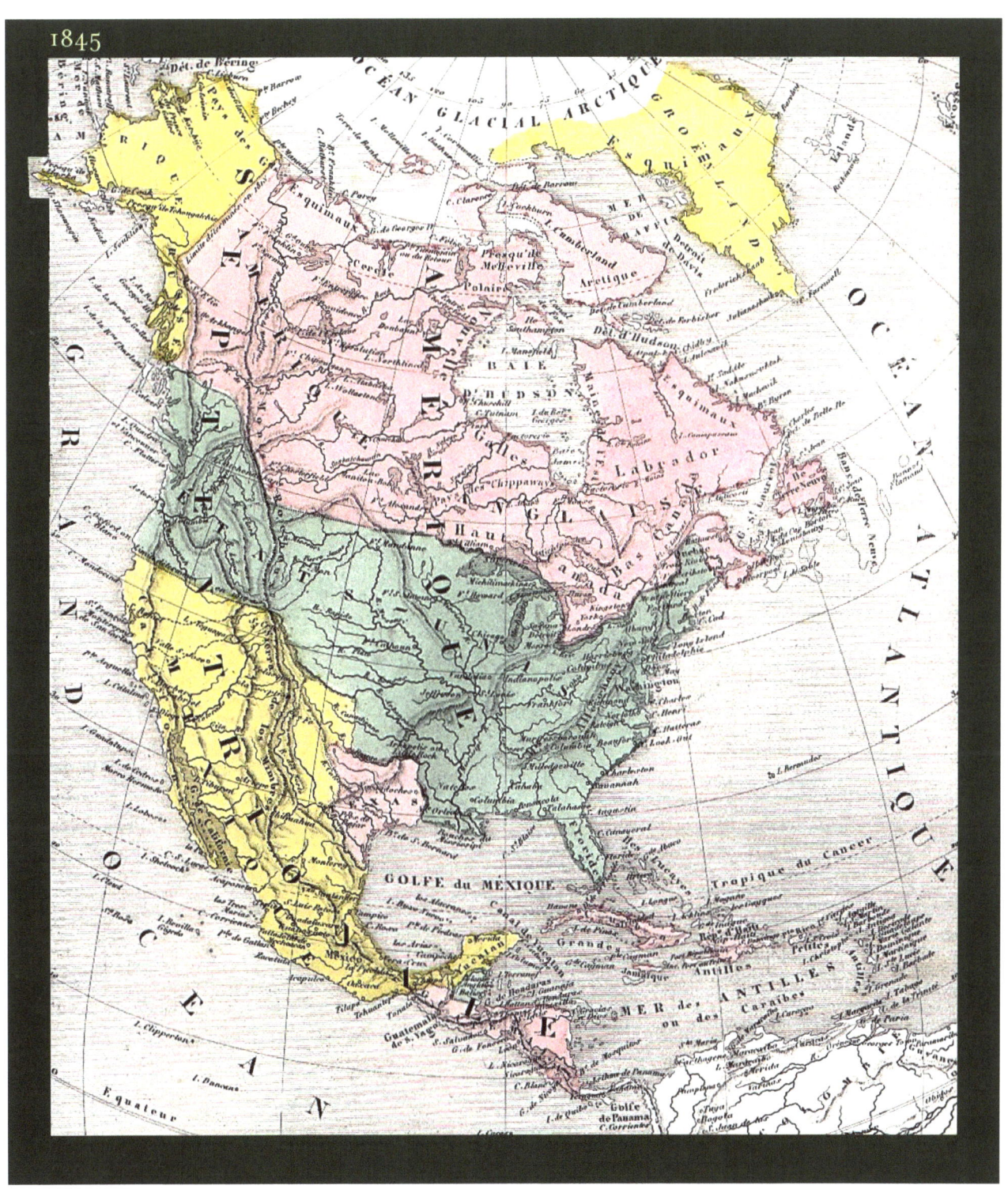

1845 Map of North America

Flags in Art

Allies Day, May, 1917
By Childe Hassam

Flags
of Oceania

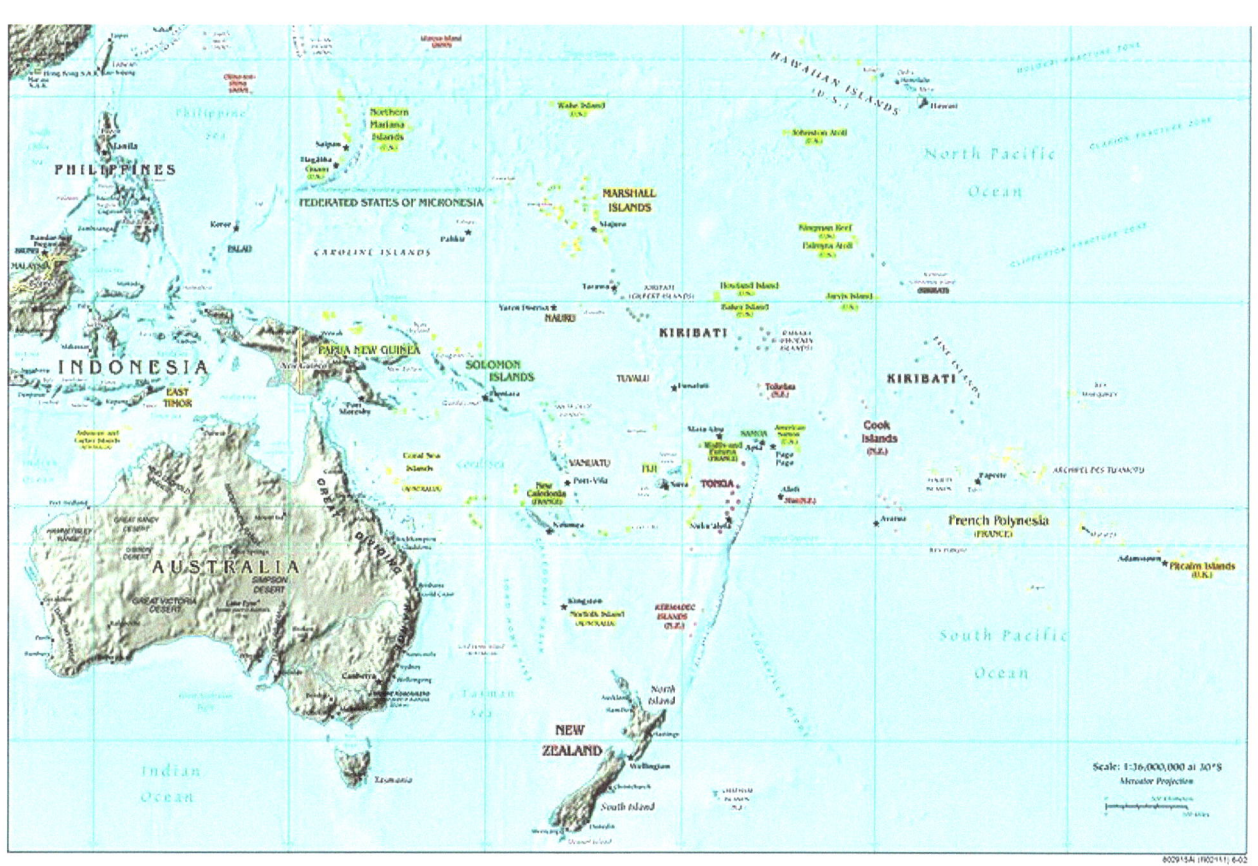

Australia

New Zealand

Countries of Melanesia:

Fiji

Indonesia

Papua New Guinea

Solomon Islands

Vanuatu

Countries of Micronesia:

Kiribati

Marshall Islands

Nauru

Countries of Polynesia:

Samoa

Tonga

Tuvalu

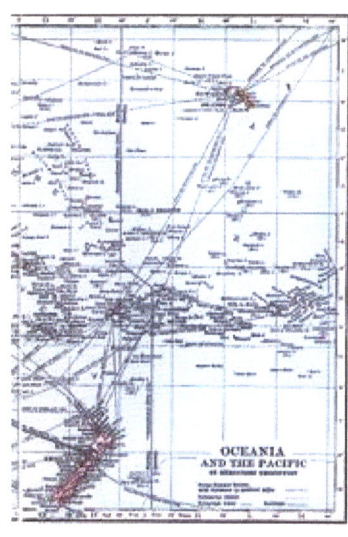

1884 Map of Oceania

Flags

of South America

Argentina

Bolivia

Brazil

Chile

Columbia

Ecuador

Guyana

Paraguay

Peru

Suriname

Uruguay

Venezuela

1892 Map of South America

Flags in Art

The Ball on Shipboard
James Tissot, 1874

Terrace at Sainte-Addresse
Claude Monet, 1867

Flag Notes:

Colors _____

_____

Shapes _____

_____

Symbols _____

_____

Words _____

_____

Other _____

_____

www.ingramcontent.com/pod-product-compliance
Lightning Source LLC
Chambersburg PA
CBHW041523280526
45792CB00004B/1353